THE POPE, PETER, GUNS, WALLS & DONALD TRUMP

Gene Keith

January 2018

This book was not written to bash Catholics. The purpose of this book is to respond to statements made by the Pope and his views on Donald Trump, guns, building walls, and other controversial issues.

All rights reserved-2018. This book may not be reproduced in any form in whole or in part without written permission from the author. For information please contact the author at gk122532@gmail.com

Scripture quotations taken from the New American Standard Bible®, Copyright © 1960, 1962, 1963, 1968, 1971, 1972, 1973, 1975, 1977, 1995 by The Lockman Foundation. Used by permission. (www.Lockman.org)

Forward

This book was not written to bash Catholics. The purpose of this book is to respond to statements made by the Pope and his views on Donald Trump, guns, building walls, and other controversial issues. For example, the Pope said:

"Donald Trump is not a Christian."

"People who manufacture or invest in guns are not Christians."

He also stated that "All religions lead to the same God."

Pope Francis also gave 1,000 priests the authority to forgive sins.

Very early in his papacy, he authorized Islamic prayers and readings from the Quran at the Vatican for the first time in history.

During a visit to St. Patrick's Cathedral in Manhattan, the Pope made it very clear that he believes that Christians and Muslims worship the same God.

And last, but not least, he spoke of a future one world religion.

We pray that God will bless you as you consider the Pope's controversial comments and our commentary on them.

Gene Keith. Gk122532@gmail.com

Table of Contents

THE POPE, PETER, GUNS, WALLS & DONALD TRUMP 1

Forward 3

Table of Contents 5

Chapter 1

Is Donald Trump a Christian? 7

Chapter 2

Are People Who Manufacture or Invest in Guns Hypocrites? 9

Chapter 3

Do All Religions Really Lead to the Same God? 15

Chapter 4

Can 1,000 Priests Forgive Sin? 23

Chapter 5

Do Christians and Muslims Worship the Same God? 29

Chapter 6

Is a Person Who Thinks Only of Building Walls a Christian? 39

Chapter 7

Peter, Popes, and the Keys to the Kingdom 41

Chapter 8

Will There Really Be a Future One World Religion? 49

Chapter 9

The Differences Between Evangelical Christians and Roman Catholics 61

About the Author 67

Chapter 1

Is Donald Trump a Christian?

The Pope said that Donald Trump was not a Christian. In an article titled, "*Is Donald Trump really a Christian? What we know about his faith,*" author Juana Summers wrote:

"Trump talks a lot about religion, but we don't know much about his own faith, or how strongly it plays a role in his personal life. He often talks about evangelicals as a group, but he also self-identifies as one."

"I am an Evangelical. I'm a Christian. I'm a Presbyterian," Trump said.

"I go to church, and I love God, and I love my church," Trump said.

But Trump said he has not asked God for forgiveness for his actions. "I am not sure I have. I just go on and try to do a better job from there."

"I think if I do something wrong, I think, I just try and make it right. I don't bring God into that picture. I don't."

He (Donald Trump) also said he receives Holy Communion.

"When I drink my little wine, which is about the only wine I drink, and have my little cracker, I guess that is a form of asking for forgiveness, and I do that as often as possible because I feel cleansed," Trump said. "I think in terms of 'let's go on and let's make it right.'"

Trump was skewered by some on the religious right for referring to a communion wafer as "my little cracker." (http://mashable.com/people/juanasummers/)

Is Donald Trump a Christian?

The Pope said that he was not.

What is your opinion?

Chapter 2

Are People Who Manufacture or Invest in Guns Hypocrites?

(http://maggiesfarm.anotherdotcom.com/uploads/Pope-on-Guns-copy.jpg)

The Pope said: "People who manufacture or invest in weapons industries are hypocrites if they call themselves Christians."

Let's Examine the Facts

The FBI estimated that 83% of Americans will be the victims of violent crime sometime during their lives. From 1973 to 1993, more Americans were murdered in their homeland than died on the battlefields of Europe and the Pacific in World War II. Two out of every five Americans are afraid to go out alone at night. What is the solution to crime in America?

Try Self Defense

There is a better way. In the opinion of this present writer, the only intelligent solution to the problem of violent crime in America is self-defense. Please allow me to state my case.

Legal Right

Citizens should never ask for their governments permission to defend themselves. Self-defense is right that is recognized by Florida law. Florida law recognizes the Castle doctrine, which is based on the premise that *"A man's home is his castle," where he may stand his ground and not retreat."*

The duty to retreat does not apply to one's home. A person assaulted in his own house or on his own premises has no duty to retreat, but may stand his ground and meet force with force, so long as the use of force appears reasonable to the reasonably prudent cautious person.

FS Chapter 776.012

Use of force in defense of person reads: "A person is justified in the use of deadly force only if he reasonably believes that such force is necessary to prevent imminent death or great bodily harm to himself or another or to prevent the imminent commission of a forcible felony."

FS Chapter 776.08

"Forcible felony means treason; murder; manslaughter; sexual battery; robbery; burglary; arson; kidnapping; aggravated assault; aggravated battery; aircraft piracy; unlawful throwing, or placing of a destructive device or bomb; and any other felony which involves the use or threat of physical force or violence against an individual."

Citizens Prevented Crimes

The crime rate would be much higher if it were not for widespread gun ownership. According to the survey by Morgan Reynolds, a scholar from Texas A & M, "armed citizens deter one million crimes each year."

Criminologist Gary Klect of FSU, has proved that there are over one million self-defense firearm uses each year, the majority of which are accomplished with handguns. His study convinced him that guns prevented many more crimes than they furthered.

99% Success Rate

Armed citizens have a 99% success rate. In studies involving armed citizens defending their homes against intruders, in only 1% of the cases did the intruder succeed in taking the gun away from the armed home owner.

Better than Police

Armed citizens are much more effective than the police. Professor Gary Klect of FSU estimated that civilians killed over 1200 felons in 1981, in shootings that were considered justifiable homicide. Citizens shot 8,600 felons (non-fatal) in 1981, or 27 justifiable shootings every day. The police killed fewer than 400 felons during the same period.

Safer than Police

Armed citizens also have a much better safety record than the police. Armed civilians mistakenly kill **30** people every year. Police mistakenly kill **330** people every year.

Guns Prevent Crimes

Armed Citizens Reduce the Crime Rate. Former Gov. Lawton Chiles pointed out that violent crime climbed about ten percent every year for much of the 1980's, but has increased less than one percent annually for the last three years. The number of arrests in Florida dropped 7.3 percent, and last year, violent crime climbed by 0.4 percent, "one of the smallest increases we've had in a number of years," said Tim Moore, Commissioner of the Florida Department of Law Enforcement (Citrus Chronicle, 3/17/94).

In the opinion of this present writer, this low rate of increase in violent crime is related to Florida's Concealed Weapon's Law that allows citizens to get a permit to carry a concealed weapon. This is the reason criminals prey on tourist rather than on Florida residents. Residents may be armed. Most tourists are not armed.

The Police Can't Protect You

Blue Lives Matter, but the police can't be there watching over us 24-7. They can come when you call but often that is too late. The crime is done, and the criminal is gone. In addition to that, did you realize that there is no constitutional duty for policemen to protect people who are not in state custody (prisoners)?

Criminals Have Rights

To make matters worse, it seems that the state is often more interested in protecting the rights of criminals than it is the rights of its citizens.

An example of this appeared in an article by Don Feder, titled, **"Brady Bill will Have No Effect on Criminals"**, In that article, Feder reminded us that:

"The U.S. Supreme Court upheld a $3 million judgment for a mugger who was shot in the back and paralyzed by a New York Transit cop after the "victim" tried to strangle a 71-year old man. It seems the officer used 'excessive force' to apprehend the assailant, this depriving him of the means of a livelihood."

Back to the Pope's Statement versus Jesus Command

"People who manufacture or invest in guns are hypocrites if they call themselves Christians."

That statement is not consistent with the teachings of Jesus that are recorded in the Bible. We challenge you to turn to the Gospel of Luke and read the account of the Lord's Supper in Luke 22.

What did Jesus Say?

Very few people realize that immediately following the Lord's Supper, the last words of Jesus to His disciples was to buy a weapon. Jesus said nothing about car payments, saving money for your children's college, or saving for retirement. But Jesus did tell His disciples to go out and buy a weapon and if they didn't have enough money to buy a weapon, to sell their clothes to raise the money and buy one. Thankfully, at least two of the disciples were smart enough to be "packing heat" at the Lord's Supper. Read it for yourself. How about you?

Read Luke 22:35-38

"And he said unto them, when I sent you without purse, and scrip, and shoes, lacked ye anything? And they said, nothing. 36 Then said he unto them, but now, he that hath a purse, let him take it, and likewise his scrip: and he that hath no sword, let him sell his garment, and buy one. 37 For I say unto you, that this that is written must yet be accomplished in me, and he was reckoned among the transgressors: for the things concerning me have an end. 38 And they said, Lord, behold, here are two swords. And he said unto them, it is enough."

The Bible says that a man who does not protect his family is worse than an infidel. The Bible says this in I Timothy 5:8 that those who don't provide for their own, especially those of their own families, have denied the faith and are worse than infidels. How can a man provide protection for his home and family without being armed? If you think you can you are deceiving yourself.

Advice from Samuel Francis

Let's face it. Unarmed citizens are as helpless as tethered sheep. Knowledgeable citizens would do well to follow the advice of Samuel Frances, who said:

"What it means is that citizens will now have to arm themselves -- not just buy a gun and keep it on their closet shelf -- but keep it on their persons.

And they will have to know how to use it when the time comes; on the commuter trains and in the fast-food places and other locations where the state has abdicated.

And, finally, it means that they will have to arm themselves, regardless of what the law says. The law of today does not protect them, and often it hurts them. So, the people are best advised to ignore the law and look out for themselves. Get a gun; learn how to use it; use it when you have to." (Samuel Francis, Power of Gun Gestapo is Fear and Ignorance, Conservative Chronicle, date missing, page 11).

The Pope said: "People who manufacture or invest in weapons industries are hypocrites if they call themselves Christians." What is your opinion?

Chapter 3

Do All Religions Really Lead to the Same God?

A video was released some time ago in which Pope Francis very clearly expressed his belief that all major religions are different paths to the same God.

He said that while people from various global faiths may be "seeking God or meeting God in different ways, that it is important to keep in mind that We are all children of God."

It appears that Pope Francis has completely abandoned any notion that a relationship with God is available only through Jesus Christ. (http://www.infowars.com/one-world-religion-pope-francis-says-all-major-religions-are-meeting-god-in-different-ways/)

Religion Will Take a Person to Hell

You may find this hard to believe but one survey indicated that 25% of the pastors in America were atheists who believe the Bible is BS.

Some Pastors Deny the Resurrection

In one survey of 7,441 Protestant pastors: 51 percent of the Methodists, 35 percent of the Presbyterians, 30 percent of the Episcopalians, and 33 percent of the American Baptists *did not believe in the physical resurrection of Jesus from the dead.*

Some Pastors Don't Believe the Bible

In another survey, 7,441 Protestant pastors were asked if they believed that the Bible is the inspired, inerrant Word of God. 87% of Methodists said NO. 95% of Episcopalians said NO. 82% of Presbyterians said NO. 67% of American Baptists said N0. (Pulpit Helps, December 1987)

Based on interviews with 601 senior pastors nationwide, representing a random cross-section of Protestant churches, George Barna reported that *only half of the country's Protestant pastors - 51% - have a biblical worldview.*
"Defining such a worldview as believing that absolute moral truth exists, that it is based upon the Bible, and having a biblical view on six core beliefs:

- The accuracy of biblical teaching,
- The sinless nature of Jesus,
- The literal existence of Satan,
- The omnipotence and omniscience of God,
- Salvation by grace alone, and
- The personal responsibility to evangelize.

The researcher produced data showing that there are significant variations by denominational affiliation and other demographics." (Google: *Barna–Biblical world view*). You may *also check out an article on biblical world view by Focus on the Family).*

The Southern Baptists had the highest percentage of pastors with a biblical worldview (71%) while the Methodists were lowest among the seven segments evaluated (27%).

There is Only One Way to God

The Bible is very clear of the fact that there is only **one way** to God and that is through the person of Jesus Christ. Read John 14:1-9.

John 14:1 "Do not let your heart be troubled; believe in God, believe also in Me.

John 14:2 "In My Father's house are many dwelling places; if it were not so, I would have told you; for I go to prepare a place for you.

John 14:3 "If I go and prepare a place for you, I will come again and receive you to Myself, that where I am, {there} you may be also.

John 14:4 "And you know the way where I am going."

John 14:5 Thomas *said to Him, "Lord, we do not know where You are going, how do we know the way?"

John 14:6 Jesus *said to him, "I am the way, and the truth, and the life; no one comes to the Father but through Me.

John 14:7 "If you had known Me, you would have known My Father also; from now on you know Him, and have seen Him."

John 14:8 ¶ Philip *said to Him, "Lord, show us the Father, and it is enough for us."

John 14:9 Jesus *said to him, "Have I been so long with you, and {yet} you have not come to know Me, Philip? He who has seen Me has seen the Father; how {can} you say, 'Show us the Father'?

Just Two Roads

Jesus said that there were just to roads leading through life. One is a wide road and the other is narrow. Jesus said that the wide road leads to death and the narrow road leads to life. Jesus also warned that most people are traveling that wide road that leads to death. The death spoken of here is hell.

Matthew 7:21 ¶ "Not everyone who says to Me, 'Lord, Lord,' will enter the kingdom of heaven, but he who does the will of My Father who is in heaven {will enter.

Matthew 7:13 ¶ "Enter through the narrow gate; for the gate is wide and the way is broad that leads to destruction, and there are many who enter through it.

Matthew 7:14 "For the gate is small and the way is narrow that leads to life, and there are few who find it.

Religious but Lost

Jesus also warned that many people were very religious but were really lost. They are hoping for heaven but were really heading for hell.

Matthew 7:22 "Many will say to Me on that day, 'Lord, Lord, did we not prophesy in Your name and in Your name cast out demons, and in Your name, perform many miracles?'

Matthew 7:23 "And then I will declare to them, 'I never knew you; DEPART FROM ME, YOU WHO PRACTICE LAWLESSNESS.'

Two Important Questions

I would like for you to give an honest answer to the following two questions.

1. Do you know for sure, that if you were to die tonight, you would go to heaven? Do you *think* you are going, *hope* you are going, *or know for sure* that you are going to heaven??

2. Suppose you died and stood before heaven's gate. As you stood there, and God asked you: **"Why should I let you into my heaven?"** What would you say?

The next words that come from your mouth will reveal to anybody who is listening, *who or what* you are depending on to keep you out of hell and get you into heaven.

I do hope that the answer you would give has nothing to do with *how good* you are; *the good things* you have done; or the *religions organizations* to which you belong.

I hope and pray that you wouldn't say, "Well! You should let me into heaven because I believe in God!"

You can't get into heaven simply *for not being an atheist*. The devil believes in God and he is going to hell. In fact, hell was made for the Devil and his angels. There are no atheists in hell because *everybody in hell believes in God.*

The Dangers of a False Hope

I am convinced, after serving in the ministry for more than fifty years, millions of people are *hoping for heaven, but heading for hell*. The sad part is, they will not know they are going to hell until it's too late!

Is the Pope Right or Wrong?

The Pope said, "While people from various global faiths may be seeking God or meeting God in different ways, that it is important to keep in mind that we are all children of God."

The Pope is dead wrong on this point.

There is only one way to God and that one way is through the person of Jesus Christ.

Chapter 4

Can 1,000 Priests Forgive Sin?

(CNN) Pope Francis has dispatched more than 1,000 "super confessors" all over the world.

The "missionaries of mercy," as the Church officially calls them, were nominated by the Pope himself, who created this new office specifically for **the** Jubilee Year of Mercy**,** which ended in November (2017).

They are priests who have been given a special license, for the duration of the Jubilee year, to forgive grave sins that usually only the Pope or top Church officials can pardon.

"This is a very strong signal from the Pope," says Mauro Cozzoli, priest and professor of moral theology at Pontifical Lateran University in Rome -- which Pope John Paul II dubbed the "University of the Pope." "He is saying that God's love is stronger than any sin."

Cozzoli says that these confessors are on a global mission to open the Church's door to repentant sinners and to Catholics who, after turning their backs on the Church, are willing to come back.

Thanks to their special powers, they can also absolve fellow priests from serious transgressions.

The grave sins that the "super confessors" can now forgive, he explained, include violence against the Pope; confessors violating the secrecy that protects confessions; unauthorized ordination of a bishop; and defiling consecrated bread and wine. (http://www.cnn.com/2016/02/12/europe/pope-francis-super-confessors/)

Can Any Priest Forgive Sin?

The idea that any priest can forgive sin is contrary to the Word of God. Only God can forgive sin. No priest can forgive sin, nor can the Pope forgive sin. Only God can forgive sin.

No Priest in the Church

To make matters worse, there is no place for a priest in the New Testament church. Read the Bible! See if you can find one example of a New Testament Church having a priest.

The officers in a true New Testament church are pastors and deacons. You will find bishops and elders, but those are simply two other words to describe the office of the pastor.

No True Apostles Today

While we are on this subject, we must warn our readers that there are no apostles in the church today. There are men who claim to be apostles, but they are false apostles. When the last of the original 12 apostles died, that office was closed.

The First Major Church Controversy

The first major doctrinal controversy to confront the early church was Montanism. This controversy concerned Divine

Revelation, the supernatural power of the Apostles, speaking in Tongues, and miracles.

About AD 150, a man named Montanus appeared in a village in Phyrgia.

Montanus claimed to be a prophet and he was accompanied by two women, Maximilla and Priscilla, who claimed to be prophetesses.

Montanus made extravagant claims. He claimed that when the twelve Apostles died, their supernatural powers and gifts were passed on to him.

He claimed that he had received direct revelations from God and that his writings superseded the writings of Paul just as Paul's writings had superseded the writings of Moses.

Montanus claimed that we were living in the last days and the New Jerusalem would descend upon his village of Pepuza in his lifetime.

Montanus and his followers spoke in tongues, exercised the gift of prophecy. He claimed that these sign gifts were "signs" of the end of the times.

So tremendous was this Montanistic movement that even Tertullian himself was swept away by its tide.

This movement was causing so much confusion in the early church, the church had to consider the questions and come up with an official decision, and decide. They did!

What was the official decision of the early church on these controversial issues?

Did the office of Apostle continue after their death?

Do all Christians receive direct and continuing revelation from God through the Holy Spirit? Did the power of the original twelve Apostles pass down to Montanus?

The Official Decision of the Early Church

The church met and addressed the questions that had led to the confusion. The church issued a decision. The decision of the Orthodox Christian Church in AD 150 is as important today as it was back then. Here is the official position of the early church.

Montanus was a heretic.

His teachings were heresy.

There were no more true Apostles. When the last Apostle died, that office was closed forever.

The Scriptures were closed. When the last verse of The Revelation was written, that was the end of God's Revelation to men.

Since the Scriptures were completed, the Holy Spirit no longer gives men "revelations" that are to be looked upon as "Scripture." The work of the Holy Spirit now is one of "illumination."

It is important to remember how early in the history of the church these controversial questions were settled. This dispute over Montanism took place while Polycarp and Papias were still alive. Those two men were disciples of John himself. John was the last of the original twelve disciples.

WARNING! MONTANISM HAS BEEN REVIVED

The tragedy of it all is that the Montanist heresy has been revived in these latter days and is causing more confusion than ever. This controversial doctrine is at the heart of the modern Charismatic movement today.

John McArthur

John McArthur made an interesting observation. He said:

"The major doctrine that Montanus have in common with modern day Charismatics is the belief that God sends new revelation on a continuing basis.

What is greatly disturbing is that they (Charistmatics) also hold this belief in common with Roman Catholics, Neo-orthodoxy (which grips many Protestant congregations today), Christian Science, the Children of God movement, Mormons, Jehovah's Witnesses, Armstrongism, and Sun-Myuung Moon, the self-styled Messiah who has duped thousands of young people in recent years."

Can 1,000 priests forgive sin?

We say "No!"

What is your opinion?

Chapter 5

Do Christians and Muslims Worship the Same God?

Very early in his papacy, Pope Francis authorized Islamic prayers at the Vatican for the first time in history.

During a visit to St. Patrick's Cathedral in Manhattan, the Pope made it very clear that he believes that Christians and Muslims worship the same God.

This is Utter Nonsense

Anyone who believes that Christians and Muslims worship the same God hasn't read the Koran or history. Christians worship Jehovah, the Creator of heaven and earth. Muslims worship Allah, the moon-god of the ancient Arabians. To make matters worse, Muslims hate Jews and Christians and they are dedicated to killing us all and establishing a caliphate over all the earth. It's time to wake up.

What Do Muslims Really Believe?

This is a very critical issue. There are Five Pillars of Islam and the first is Affirmation: "There is no God but Allah, and Muhammad is his messenger."

The Bible says the same thing about Jehovah. The very First Commandment establishes the fact that there is only One True and living God. "And God spake all these words, saying, I am the LORD thy God, which have brought thee out of the land of Egypt, out of the house of bondage. Thou shalt have no other gods before me." (Exodus 20:1-2)

Who is Allah?

In ancient Arabia, long before Mohammad was born, the dominant religion of that day was *Sabianism*, which was the worship of the sun, moon, and stars.

Every Arab tribe had its sacred, magic stones, which the Arabians believed, protected their tribes. Mohammad's tribe had adopted a black stone. That stone was probably an asteroid or a meteorite that had fallen from heaven - and the *Arabs believed it to be divine.*

The Arabs believed the moon was a *male deity*, and a lunar calendar was used. Their pagan fasting would begin on the crescent moon.

Allah was the moon god and he was represented by the black stone that had come down from heaven. Allah (the moon god) was worshiped by the Arabs long before Mohammad came along.

The Arabs of that day also believed the sun was the female goddess. They believed that Allah, the moon god married the sun goddess, and they gave birth to the three daughters of Allah.

When Mohammad came along, there were 360 different (demon) gods worshiped by the Arabians and moon and the sun topped the list. When Mohammad took control of Mecca he destroyed all idols except Allah, the moon god, who was represented by the black stone.

In the days before Islam, the *symbol of the moon god, Allah, was the crescent.* It was common throughout the Middle East today. The crescent moon can be seen on every Islamic flag, in every Mosque, and even on the hats of men who belong to the Order of the Mystic Shrine.

Mohammad

Mohammad, the founder of Islam, was born in 570 A.D. and died at the age of 62.

Mohammad was a camel driver until the age of 25 when he married an older woman who was quite wealthy. For the next 15 years, Mohammad and his wife ran a fruit business.

When Mohammad was 40 years old he began going into a cave to meditate. This cave was about 3 miles north of Mecca. While praying and meditating in that cave, Mohammad would go into, what some describe as epileptic seizures (fits). He would shake; he would perspire, and he would foam at the mouth. Some believe he suffered from epilepsy. Others believe Mohammad was experiencing demon possession.

According to Muslim tradition, while Mohammad was meditating in that cave near Mecca, the **angel Gabriel appeared** to Mohammad and gave him several special revelations.

Those revelations were not written down in a book called the "Koran" until years later because Mohammad was uneducated and probably did not know how to read or write.

Among those revelations are the belief that:

Allah was the one true god. He created everything.

Man is God's slave. The chief duty of man is to submit to god. The word "Islam" means: submission.

There will be a day of judgement. Man will be saved or lost depending on his good deeds (works).

Gabriel also told Mohammad that he was to loot and steal from the caravans that were passing through and that he was to kill the men.

The Koran reports that Mohammad fought many battles and killed tens of thousands of people.

Gabriel also told Mohammad to kill and drive out all Jews. At one time, Mohammad caught 1,000 Jewish men, brought them together, and had them beheaded.

In another revelation, Gabriel told Mohammad that Islam was to be exalted above all other religions, including Judaism and Christianity. Therefore, Islam is known the world over as "the religion of the sword." Today, 1/6 of the world's population practices this religion.

According to Muslim law, there is mandatory death penalty for anyone who defiles the name of the Islamic prophet Mohammad. (Gainesville Sun, Saturday, May 9, 1998).

THE DANGER OF WORSHIPING ALLAH

1. The worship of Allah violates the First Commandment which prohibits worshiping any God but Jehovah. God's Word is very clear on this!

(Exodus 20:1-2) "I am Jehovah your God who liberated you from your slavery in Egypt. You may worship **no other God** but me."

(Deuteronomy 6:4-5) "Hear, O Israel: The Lord our **God is One Lord** and though shalt love the lord thy God with all thine heart and with all thy soul and with all thy might."

(Exodus 20:3) "Thou shalt have **no other gods** before me."

2. The worship of Allah violates the Second Commandment that prohibits worshiping images or objects. Allah was represented by a <u>black stone</u>.

(Exodus 20:4-5) "You shall not make yourselves any <u>idols</u>: any images resembling animals, birds, or fish. You must never bow to an image or worship it in any way; for I, the Lord your god, am very possessive. I will not share my affection with any other god."

3. The worship of Allah is idolatry. It violates the Commandment that warns against worshiping the "host of heaven."

(Deuteronomy 4:19) "And do not look up into the sky to worship **the sun, moon, or stars**. The Lord may permit the other nations to get away with this, but not you."

(2 Kings 21:3-5) "He built heathen alters to the sun god, **moon god,** and the gods of the stars."

3. To worship Allah is to worship Satan because Satan is behind all false religion.

(1 Corinthians 10:19-20) 19 "What am I trying to say? Am I saying that the idols to whom the pagans bring sacrifices are real gods and that these sacrifices are of some value?

20 No, not at all. What I am saying is that these sacrifices are offered to demons, not to God. And I don't want any of you to be partners with demons. (NLT)

(II Corinthians 4:3-4) 3 If the Good News we preach is veiled from anyone, it is a sign that they are perishing.

4 Satan, the god of this evil world, has blinded the minds of those who don't believe, so they are unable to see the glorious light of the Good News that is shining upon them

(II Corinthians 11:14) "But I am not surprised! Even Satan can disguise himself as an angel of light."

Don Walton reminded us that The Devil is behind all false religions and that Satan's purpose is twofold.

1. First: By hiding behind false religions, Satan becomes the indirect recipient of man's worship. Unknown to them, when the adherents of false religions worship their gods they are really *worshiping Satan*.

2. Second: Satan masterfully uses false religions to keep men from the one and only True God.

Of all false religions in the world today, none is a more formidable foe to the Christian faith than Islam. Walton also reminds us that, 'according to Paul, when the world falls down at the feet of false gods it is really before Satan, the god of this world."

Islam and The Order of the Mystic Shrine

Have you ever been to a parade where members of the Shrine Club were present, and were driving their funny cars? Did you look closely at those hats they were wearing? Do you have any idea what those hats stand for and where those symbols came from? Those caps are called Fezes, and were named after a city named Fez.

Many years ago (8th century) in Morocco, there was a Christian community named Fez. One day, a horde of Muslims terrorists swooped down upon that Christian community and *slaughtered every Christian in the city.*

The Muslims were shouting "There is no god but Allah and Muhammad his prophet." The Muslims literally butchered every born-again Christian in that city.

During the butchering of the people of Fez, the streets literally ran red with the blood of martyred Christians. The Muslim murderers dipped their caps in the blood of their victims as a testimony to Allah. Those blood-stained caps eventually were called "fezzes" and became a badge of honor for those who had killed a Christian.

Today, members of the Shrine Club wear that same fez today, with the Islamic sword and crescent encrusted with jewels. The tragedy is that many are worn by men who profess to be Christians themselves.

Shiners' Blood Oath

When a member of the *Order of the Mystic Shrine* is initiated at the Alter of Obligation, he must bow in worship, with his hands tied behind his back, and proclaim Allah (the demon god) to be the god of his fathers.

The Shriners' blood oath and confession of Allah as God is documented in the secret lodge document, THE MYSTIC SHRINE: An Illustrated Ritual of the Ancient Arabic Order of Nobles of the Shrine, 1975 edition (pages 20-22).

(Carlson & Decker, "Fast Facts about False Teachings," Eugene, Oregon: Harvest House. 1994.)

Summary

Muslims and Christians do not worship the same God. Christians worship Jehovah, the Creator of heaven and the earth. Muslims worship Allah, the moon god of the ancient Arabians.

Islam is seductive. It is attracting young militants from all over the world (even in America), and especially in our prison system. In ten years (2017), it is predicted that 50 percent of the Russian military will be Muslims.

We also believe that Islam will be the false religious system that will "head up" the apostate religious system of the Great Tribulation. We will explain this in chapter 8.

Chapter 6

Is a Person Who Thinks Only of Building Walls a Christian?

The picture above is the Vatican where Pope Francis lives. No comment needed. A picture is worth 1,000 words.

Chapter 7

Peter, Popes, and the Keys to the Kingdom

Roman Catholics believe that Simon Peter was the first Pope and that the church was built on Peter. What does the Bible teach on this controversial subject? Was Peter the first Pope? Let's examine those claims.

Was the Church Built on Peter?

Was the church built on Peter?" Roman Catholics believe that the church was built on Peter. What does the Bible say?

(Matthew 16:16-18) "16 And Simon Peter answered and said, Thou art the Christ, the Son of the living God.

17 And Jesus answered and said unto him, Blessed art thou, Simon Barjona: for flesh and blood hath not revealed it unto thee, but my Father which is in heaven.

18 And I say also unto thee, 'That thou art Peter, and upon this rock I will build my church; and the gates of hell shall not prevail against it.' "(KJV)

Jesus is the Cornerstone

(Ephesians 2:19-20) 19 "Now therefore ye are no more strangers and foreigners, but fellow citizens with the saints, and of the household of God;

20 And are built upon the foundation of the apostles and prophets, Jesus Christ himself being the chief corner stone."

The Apostles were the Foundation

The church was built on Jesus. Peter and the other Apostles were a part of the foundation. The Apostles got in on the ground floor. Peter was an Apostle, but he was just one of the twelve. Jesus took that material (Peter and the other Apostles) and "poured the foundation" for His Church. The church today is composed of people from every tribe and nation who believe what Peter believed and confessed.

What about Priests?

There is not a word in the New Testament about human priests, much less Popes. This is based entirely on Catholic tradition, not the Bible. In addition to that, there are other Biblical and historical problems with the idea of Peter being the first Pope.

Biblical Facts about Peter

There is no evidence that Peter ever set foot in the city of Rome, much less served as the first Pope.

Peter Was Married

Roman Catholics believe Peter was the first Pope. The first problem we must deal with is that Peter was married. Priests and Popes are not married.

Peter had a Mother-in-Law

In Mark 1:29:31, we read of Jesus healing Peter's mother-in-law of a fever. She was healed and then had to get up and fix supper for the disciples. (No rest for the weary).

29 And forthwith, when they were come out of the synagogue, they entered into the house of Simon and Andrew, with James and John.

30 But Simon's wife's mother lay sick of a fever, and immediately they spoke to Jesus about her.

31 And he came and took her by the hand, and lifted her up; and immediately the fever left her, and she ministered unto them."

Peter's Wife Traveled with Him

Not only did Peter have a wife, the Bible says that she traveled with Peter as he went on his preaching tours.

(I Corinthians 9:4-5) 4 Have we not power to eat and to drink?

 5 Have we not power to lead about a sister, a wife, as well as other apostles, and as the brethren of the Lord, and Cephas (Peter)?"

James was the Leader of the Jerusalem Church

Read Acts 15. Peter was used greatly of God, but he was never recognized as the "Head of the church."

Paul Publicly Rebuked Peter for his Racism

Read Galatians 2:14. If Peter was the Pope, Paul would not have rebuked him.

Peter's Ministry was to the Jews - Paul went to the Gentiles
Read Galatians 2:7-10. Did you know that there is no evidence at all that Peter ever visited Rome, much less served as Pope there?

(Romans 15:16) Paul wrote this to the Gentile Romans: "That I should be the minister of Jesus Christ to the Gentiles, ministering the gospel of God, that the offering up of the Gentiles might be acceptable."

(Galatians 2:7) "But contrariwise, when they saw that the gospel of the uncircumcision (Gentiles) was committed unto me [Paul], as the gospel of the circumcision (Jews and the other tribes of Israel), was unto Peter."

Peter Wrote the book of I Peter from Literal Babylon
One of the reasons some place Peter in Rome, is from the book of First Peter, chapter five, verse thirteen. Protestant tradition teaches that "Babylon" was a code word for "Rome." Those who hold to that tradition also believe the Roman Catholic Church is the apostate church, called the great harlot in Revelation, chapters 17 and 18. This writer does not subscribe to that theory.

(I Peter 5:13) "The church that is at Babylon, elected together with you, saluteth you; and so doth Marcus my son." (KJV)

Babylon is Literal Babylon - Not Rome

Peter wrote his letter from Babylon (Iraq). Babylon is Babylon and Rome is Rome! As we stated before, Peter was the Apostle to the Jews (referred to as the circumcision) and Paul was the Apostle to the Gentiles.

Peter ministered where Jews were and there were thousands of Jews in Iraq when he wrote his letter from there. In fact, there were two Jewish Universities in Babylon in those days.

Why Didn't Paul Mention Peter?

When Paul concluded his letter to the Romans, he specifically mentioned 35 people. Why didn't he mention Peter? He didn't mention Peter because Perter was not in Rome.

Romans 16:1 I commend to you our sister **Phoebe**, who is a servant of the church which is at **Cenchrea;**

Romans 16:2 that you receive her in the Lord in a manner worthy of the saints, and that you help her in whatever matter she may have need of you; for she herself has also been a helper of many, and of myself as well.

Romans 16:3 ¶ Greet **Prisca and Aquila**, my fellow workers in Christ Jesus,

Rom 16:4 who for my life risked their own necks, to whom not only do I give thanks, but also all the churches of the Gentiles;

Romans 16:5 also {greet} the church that is in their house. Greet **Epaenetus,** my beloved, who is the first convert to Christ from Asia.

Romans 16:6 Greet **Mary**, who has worked hard for you.

Romans 16:7 Greet **Andronicus and Junias**, my kinsmen and my fellow prisoners, who are outstanding among the apostles, who also were in Christ before me.

Romans 16:8 Greet **Ampliatus**, my beloved in the Lord.

Romans 16:9 Greet **Urbanus,** our fellow worker in Christ, and **Stachys** my beloved.

Romans 16:10 Greet **Apelles**, the approved in Christ. Greet those who are of the {household} of **Aristobulus.**

Romans 16:11 Greet **Herodion**, my kinsman. Greet those of the {household} of **Narcissus**, who are in the Lord.

Romans 16:12 Greet **Tryphaena and Tryphosa**, workers in the Lord. Greet Persis the beloved, who has worked hard in the Lord.

Romans 16:13 Greet **Rufus**, a choice man in the Lord, also **his mother** and mine.

Romans 16:14 Greet **Asyncritus, Phlegon, Hermes, Patrobas, Hermas** and the brethren with them.

Romans 16:15 Greet **Philologus and Julia, Nereus and his sister**, and **Olympas**, and all the saints who are with them.

Romans 16:16 Greet one another with a holy kiss. All the churches of Christ greet you.

Romans 16:17 ¶ Now I urge you, brethren, keep your eye on those who cause dissensions and hindrances contrary to the teaching which you learned, and turn away from them.

Romans 16:18 For such men are slaves, not of our Lord Christ but of their own appetites; and by their smooth and flattering speech they deceive the hearts of the unsuspecting.

Romans 16:19 For the report of your obedience has reached to all; therefore, I am rejoicing over you, but I want you to be wise in what is good and innocent in what is evil.

Romans 16:20 The God of peace will soon crush Satan under your feet. ¶ The grace of our Lord Jesus be with you.

Romans 16:21 ¶ Timothy my fellow worker greets you, and {so} {do} **Lucius and Jason and Sosipater**, my kinsmen.

Romans 16:22 ¶ I, **Tertius**, who write this letter, greet you in the Lord.

Romans 16:23 ¶ **Gaius**, host to me and to the whole church, greets you. **Erastus**, the city treasurer greets you, and **Quartus**, the brother.

Romans 16:24 The grace of our Lord Jesus Christ be with you all. Amen.

What About the Keys to the Kingdom?

Didn't we read in Matthew 16:19 that Jesus gave Peter the "Keys to the Kingdom?" Yes, He did! And Peter used those keys on two historical occasions.

Matthew 16:17-19

17 And Jesus answered and said unto him, Blessed art thou, Simon Barjona: for flesh and blood hath not revealed it unto thee, but my Father which is in heaven.

18 And I say also unto thee, that thou art Peter, and upon this rock I will build my church; and the gates of hell shall not prevail against it.

19 And I will give unto thee the keys of the kingdom of heaven: and whatsoever thou shalt bind on earth shall be bound in heaven: and whatsoever thou shalt loose on earth shall be loosed in heaven."

Peter's Used the Keys Twice

Peter used those keys the first time on the Day of Pentecost. God used him to open the door to the JEWS. On that day, Peter preached a powerful sermon and 3000 new converts became a part of the New Testament church. You can read the entire story in Acts 2.

Peter's Used the Keys in Acts 10

Peter used the keys the second time in Acts 10, when he opened the door of the church to the Gentiles. Peter was sent to the home of an Italian Army officer named Cornelius. While Peter was preaching, the Holy Spirit fell on Cornelius and the people gathered there. Peter was astonished to learn that Gentiles could be saved as well as the Jews.

When Peter went back to the church in Jerusalem, he was called on the carpet for preaching to Gentiles. It takes the entire chapter of Acts 11 for the church to understand what God had done through Peter.

Chapter 8

Will There Really Be a Future One World Religion?

As he has done throughout his papacy, the Pope continues to lay the groundwork for the coming one world religion, and yet hardly anyone seems to be upset by this.

The Coming New World Order

While most of us have been asleep or have had our heads buried in the sand, the world has been steadily moving towards what some call, "The New World Order."

The United Nations & Agenda 21

The United Nations is working night and day to establish a one world government. If there is any doubt in your mind ab out this, you should read the following three books that are available on Amazon.com.

Public Schools

Did you realize that the idea of a one world government is taught in every public school in America? The official philosophy of every government school in America is secular humanism. There are five basic doctrines to humanism and doctrine five is a "socialist one world government."

Those who question that public schools are teaching Socialism and a one-world government should consider the remarks by

Chester Pierce, made while giving a seminar on childhood education at Harvard in 1973.

"Every child in America entering school at the age of age five is mentally ill, because he comes to school with certain allegiances toward our founding fathers, toward our elected officials, toward his parents, toward a belief in a supernatural Being, toward the sovereignty of this nation as a separate entity. <u>It's up to you teachers to make all of these sick children well by creating the international child of the future.</u>" (Chester Pierce was a professor of Educational Psychiatry in Harvard in 1973)

The United Nations Influence on Our Schools

"This educational reform initiative is evident in the UNESCO program called **"United Nations' Decade of Education for Sustainable Development."**

It is their stated goal in this program to steal one generation of children and teach them to place loyalty to the state above loyalty to the family.

Once this objective has been realized, it is a simple task to then inculcate the children with the basic tenets of sustainable development. These tenets include:

The end of national sovereignty.

The abolition of private property.

The restructuring of the family unit.

Restriction of individual mobility and opportunity.

The abandonment of constitutional rights.

The relocation of people into smart growth zones. (Taylor, Ron. Agenda 21: An Expose of the United Nations' Sustainable Development Initiative and the Forfeiture of American Sovereignty and Liberties (With Important 2030 Agenda Updates) (Kindle Locations 393-403).

What Does the Bible Teach on This?

The Bible clearly teaches that final days of history, there will be a "one world" religion and a "one-world government.

There will also be a "one-world ruler (dictator) known as the Anti-Christ.

This world dictator will come to power, partly with the assistance of a false religious system which is described in detail in Revelation, chapters 17-18.

This system is described as a harlot riding on a scarlet colored beast. This image of a woman riding a beast can be seen today in the front of the European Union building in Brussels.

Who is This Woman?

As we stated, the beast represents the future one-world government and the harlot riding the beast represents the one-world false religion of that period. For as long as this writer can remember, protestant writers and speakers have been unanimous in their belief that this woman is the Catholic Church. This belief has been a part of our tradition for so long, that today, it is accepted without question or reservation.

Rejected Traditional View

Where is the evidence that supports the traditional view that identifies the Catholic Church as the "mystery woman" and the "great harlot" of The Revelation? When I began to do a serious study on this subject, I experienced a rude awakening. I began to have serious reservations with the traditional position. I then rejected the traditional view totally and embraced a totally different interpretation. I believe the one world false religion of the future is Islam, not Roman Catholicism.

WHAT WE BELIEVE

1. The very next event on God's prophetic calendar is the Rapture of the church. Many popular leaders reject this. We will explain this at the end of this chapter.

2. This is followed by a seven-year period known as the Great Tribulation, during which the world government and the one world false religion will appear. Read II Thessalonians 2 for a complete outline of these important events. Chapter 2 through chapter 19 in the Revelation cover this same period in detail.

3. We believe the one world false religion is Islam, not the Roman Catholic Church.

4. Islam is a false religion. Allah is the "moon god" of pagan Arabs.

5. Islam hates Christianity, calls Christians and Jews infidels and kills them today.

6. Islam believes in forced conversion.

7. Islam is more than a religion. It is also a system of world government.

8. Islam is reported to be the fastest growing religion in the world, especially in American prisons.

9. When all true believers are removed from the earth prior to the tribulation, there will be no power on earth to prevent Islam from taking over the whole (lost) world.

10. Muslims hate Israel and refuse to even acknowledge her right to exist.

The late Dr. Vernon McGee said: "The Great Harlot is that part of the church that will remain after the true church has been raptured."

This false religion will be composed of those who have never trusted Christ as their Savior. This is the group that enters the Great Tribulation.

All Atheists will be left behind.

All unsaved members from every church and from every denomination will be left behind.

All unsaved pastors, priests, and popes will be left behind.

All Pantheists who worship nature and "mother earth" will be left behind.

All Polytheist who worship many gods will be left behind.

All unsaved Evolutionist who have rejected God as Creator and worship the god of junk science and believe everything in the universe (matter, plant life, animal life, and man) are the result of the great scientific formula: Nothing x Time x Chance = Everything, will be left behind.

All Animist and Spiritists who communicate with demons who pose as spirit guides will be left behind.

All who believe in astrology and worship the zodiac and believe the heavenly bodies (stars, etc.) control events on earth, will be left behind.

All unsaved Humanist who dethrone God and exalt man. The millions of people who blindly follow the religious systems of the world will be left behind.

All unsaved Masons, Knights of Columbus, and members of the Order of the Mystic Shrine will be left behind.

All unsaved Mormons. All unsaved members of the various cults will be left behind.

All of those people will be left behind when Christ comes for His Church.

All devout Muslims who worship Allah and hate Christians and Jews, will be left behind.

At that point, they will all come together and form a one-world religion.

For more detailed information on these three theories we suggest you order my book, **"You Can Understand the Revelation."** It is available on Amazon.com in print and in the Kindle format.

YOU CAN UNDERSTAND THE REVELATION

FOUR POPULAR INTERPRETATIONS

GENE KEITH

Warning!! Many Reject Our Position

To be fair with our readers we must warn you that there are scores of pastors, professors, and popular religious leaders who reject what we have just written. We cover those different positions in the book pictured above.

The Preterist (Past) Position

The word, "praeter" means past. Therefore, those holding the Preterist view believe that Daniel and the Revelation were fulfilled in the past.

According to Preterism, events like the rise of the Antichrist, the Tribulation, the Second Coming of Christ, and the Day of the Lord, all took place around 70 A.D., the year the Romans invaded Jerusalem and destroyed the second Temple.

Partial Preterist

There are four different groups of Preterist, but Partial Preterists are the most popular. Prominent Partial Preterists include Gary DeMar, R.C. Sproul, Ken Gentry, and The Bible Answerman, Hank Hanegraaff.

Partial Preterists believe in a second coming and the resurrection of believers and the judgment seat of Christ. But Partial Preterists **do not believe in the Rapture, a literal Millennium, the Battle of Armageddon, a literal Anti-Christ, or a role for national Israel.**

Summary

We invite our readers to "pick their seat and ride." If you believe Jesus returned in A.D. 70, and that there will be no Rapture, Tribulation, or literal kingdom, then go ahead and believe it.

However, we believe that the next thing on God's prophetic calendar is the Rapture of the church, followed by the Great Tribulation and the coming New World Order.

We believe that the only power on earth today that is holding this back is the Holy Spirit, who dwells in the bodies of believers. Please take the time to read II Thessalonians 2 as you consider what you have just read.

II Thessalonians 2 (Living Bible)

1-2 And now, what about the coming again of our Lord Jesus Christ and our being gathered together to meet him?

Please don't be upset and excited, dear brothers, by the rumor that this day of the Lord has already begun. If you hear of people having visions and special messages from God about this, or letters that are supposed to have come from me, don't believe them.

3 Don't be carried away and deceived regardless of what they say. For that day will not come until two things happen: first, there will be a time of great rebellion against God, and then the man of rebellion will come— the son of hell.

4 He will defy every god there is and tear down every other object of adoration and worship. He will go in and sit as God in the temple of God, claiming that he himself is God.

5 Don't you remember that I told you this when I was with you?

6 And you know what is keeping him from being here already; for he can come only when his time is ready.

7 As for the work this man of rebellion and hell will do when he comes, it is already going on, but he himself will not come until the one who is holding him back steps out of the way.

8 Then this wicked one will appear, whom the Lord Jesus will burn up with the breath of his mouth and destroy by his presence when he returns.

9 This man of sin will come as Satan's tool, full of satanic power, and will trick everyone with strange demonstrations, and will do great miracles.

10 He will completely fool those who are on their way to hell because they have said no to the Truth; they have refused to believe it and love it and let it save them,

11 so God will allow them to believe lies with all their hearts,

12 and all of them will be justly judged for believing falsehood, refusing the Truth, and enjoying their sins.

13 But we must forever give thanks to God for you, our brothers loved by the Lord, because God chose from the very first to give you salvation, cleansing you by the work of the Holy Spirit and by your trusting in the Truth.

14 Through us he told you the Good News. Through us he called you to share in the glory of our Lord Jesus Christ.

15 With all these things in mind, dear brothers, stand firm and keep a strong grip on the truth that we taught you in our letters and during the time we were with you.

16 May our Lord Jesus Christ himself and God our Father, who has loved us and given us everlasting comfort and hope, which we don't deserve,

17 comfort your hearts with all comfort, and help you in every good thing you say and do." (Inc. Tyndale House Publishers. The Living Bible (Kindle Locations 52172-52201). Tyndale House Publishers. Kindle Edition)

Chapter 9

The Differences Between Evangelical Christians and Roman Catholics

We want to stress again that this book was not written to bash Catholics. The purpose of this book is to answer some serious questions and to point out the differences between a Bible-believing New Testament Church and the modern Roman Catholic Church.

There Are Some Things on Which We Both Agree

Evangelical Christians and Roman Catholics both believe in the Virgin Birth.

Evangelical Christians and Roman Catholics both believe in the Deity of Christ.

Evangelical Christians and Roman Catholics both believe in the death, burial, and resurrection of Jesus Christ.

Evangelical Christians and Roman Catholics both believe the Bible.

Both Evangelical Christians and Roman Catholics usually are pro-life.

However, there are several areas in which Evangelical Christians and Roman Catholics do not agree.'

The True Church
Most Catholics believe they are the one true church and that the Roman Catholic Church was built on Peter. We don't believe that.

Pope Peter
Most Catholics also believe that Peter was the First Pope and that there is an unbroken "chain of command" from Peter until the present time. Good Catholics believe that the word of the Pope is equal to the Word of God. They believe the Pope is the representative of Christ on earth and when he speaks "from the chair," his word is equal to the Word of God. We don't believe that.

The Apocrypha
We believe the 66 books of the Old and New Testaments. Catholics also believe a collection of writings called the Apocrypha (which, by the way, were included in the original King James Translation of the Bible).

The Priesthood
Catholics believe in an official priesthood. People come to the priest, confess their sins, and find forgiveness. We don't find the office of priest mentioned in the epistles written to the church. The New Testament Church has pastors and deacons, not priests. In fact, there is no provision for the office of priest in the Christian religion.

Mary
We believe Mary was a virgin until Jesus was born. Catholics believe Mary maintained her virginity (perpetual virginity)

and the brothers of Jesus were probably the children of Joseph by another woman. Catholics also believe that Mary was sinless and that she can influence Jesus when we pray through her.

The Bible Plus Tradition

The major differences between the New Testament Church and the Roman Catholic Church is tradition. We believe the Bible alone. Catholics believe the Bible plus many man-made traditions.

THE MAJOR DIFFERENCES

The major difference between a New Testament Church and the Roman Catholic Church is that we base our doctrines on the Bible and the Bible alone. Roman Catholics base their doctrines on the Bible, the Apocrypha, and man-made traditions.

Jesus warned about this in (Matthew 15:6) "You have made the Commandment of God of none effect by your tradition." Here are several examples of man-made traditions.

Mother of God

Mary's title "Mother of God" was made official and incorporated in prayers at the third Ecumenical Council in Ephesus (Turkey) in 431.

Immaculate Conception

In 1854, Pope Pius IX declared that Mary was preserved from original sin.

The Assumption

In 1950, the year this writer graduated from high school, Pope Pius XII declared when Mary died, she was taken up, body and soul, to heaven.

Redemption

Roman Catholics believe Mary participates in the redemption achieved by her son.

Mary's Intercession

Catholics believe that all Graces that flow from the suffering and death of Jesus Christ are granted only through Mary's intercession with her son.

Prayer

Roman Catholics believe all prayers and petitions from the faithful on earth must likewise flow through Mary, who then brings them to the attention of Jesus.

The New Testament Church

The Biblical New Testament church has pastors, elders, and deacons. The Catholic Church has priests and popes.

Pastors must be the husband of one wife. Priests cannot marry. See I Timothy 3 for the qualifications of church leaders.

Pastors' children must be well-behaved. Priests have no children. (I Timothy 3)

We believe all believers are saints. Catholics elevate certain people to sainthood.

We believe Mary was a virgin until Jesus was born. Roman Catholics believe in perpetual virginity.

We believe baptism is symbolic. Catholics believe baptism is essential to salvation.

We baptize believers only. Catholics baptize infants.

We believe the Lord's Supper is a memorial. They believe it literally becomes the blood and body of Jesus.

We believe in heaven and hell. Catholics believe in purgatory.

WHAT THE LAST POPE BELIEVED ABOUT PURGATORY

By Moody Adams

In his August 4, 1999 General Audience, speaking about purgatory, Pope Paul II said: "We cannot approach God without undergoing some kind of purification." (The Pope included himself by the choice of the word "We").

The Pope explained this purification comes through purgatory: "Every trace of attachment to evil must be eliminated, every imperfection of the soul corrected. Purification must be complete." Indeed, this is precisely what is meant by the Church's teaching on purgatory?
(http://www.thecatholicfaith.com/Teachings/purgatory.htm)

John Paul II declared purgatory is taught in the Old and New Testaments as a means of purifying the soul. Catholic doctrine states that in purgatory fires burns Christians until the flames have thoroughly cleansed them, Purgatory (Lat., "purgare", to make clean, to purify) in accordance with Catholic teaching is a place or condition of temporal punishment ... the existence of an intermediate state in which the dross of lighter transgressions will be burnt away, and the soul thus purified will be saved.? **(http://www.newadvent.org/cathen/12575a.htm#I)**

The Pope would be saved if he repented of his sins and trusted in the finished work of Jesus Christ. You can be saved if you repent of your sins and trust in the finished work of Jesus Christ.

You don't have to go through a priest. Now you can go directly to God. And you don't have to burn in purgatory.

Is there any good reason why you can't be saved right now?

If you believe that you are a sinner; and that Jesus died for you; and you are willing to repent of your sins and trust Him, you can be saved.

About the Author

Gene Keith was born William Eugene Keith in Tarpon Springs, Florida, on December 25, 1932. His parents were Walter Keith Jr. and Louise (Campbell) Keith.

Gene graduated from Tarpon Springs High School in 1950, and married his sweetheart, Tuelah Evelyn Riviere in 1952. Her parents were Lawrence and Viola Riviere.

Gene became a Christian in 1952 and entered the ministry in 1953.

Florida Baptist Witness

(Circling the Wagons, which appeared in the Florida Baptist Witness January 28, 2013 Joni B. Hannigan, Managing Editor).

"Gene Keith is part of a ten-generation legacy of pioneer Christian leaders from Kentucky, Texas, and Florida. Since 1773 when John Keith hosted the first meeting of Virginia's Ten Mile Baptist Church, the Keith men for at least ten generations have led their congregations as Baptist preachers, elders or deacons, to be pioneers in sharing the Gospel.

By wagon, on horseback, on foot, and by car, they've traveled carrying the Good News of Christ from the thick forests of Virginia, across the green mountains of Kentucky, to the High Plains of Texas before finally turning back southeast to settle in sun-drenched Central Florida where three generations now pastor two churches just 20 miles apart. Gene has served as pastor in Taft, Otter Creek, Gainesville twice, and as the Pastor of the First Baptist Church of Cape Canaveral, Florida in 1968-1969, when America sent the first Astronauts to the moon.

Gene has many years of experience in broadcasting, not only as a "DJ," but also including his own daily "talk show" type program known as "The Sound of Inspiration," which was popular on several radio stations in North Central Florida. He was also a DJ from 2-6 pm weekdays on the first FM Country Music station in Gainesville.

Gene attended Stetson University, the University of Florida, and received his BA from Luther Rice College and Seminary. He has many years of experience in the Christian School movement.

He is the founder of the Countryside Christian School which celebrated its 43nd anniversary in 2017. He has experience as a pastor and a Christian School Principal. Gene also served as a Consultant and Field Representative for Accelerated Christian Education. During that time, he helped establish several other Christian Schools in Florida. Many of his family are involved in education serving as school Principals, teachers and coaches.

Gene also has experience in the political arena. He has run for the office of State Senator, The Florida House of Representatives, and The United States Congress. In one election, he lost by one percentage point (499 votes).

Gene has traveled to many of the popular places including England, France, Germany, Italy, Greece, and especially Israel. Gene spent a week in Israel immediately following the Six-Day War in 1967.

Many in Gene's family are involved in health care. His aunt, Charlotte (Palmer) Campbell was the first woman to graduate from the University of Florida School of Pharmacy. Several of Gene's grandchildren are involved in health care, serving as Office Managers, Surgery Coordinators, nurses, and transporters. Gene's family is represented in the NFR Hospital, Shands Teaching Hospital, and the UF Orthopedic Center in Gainesville.

Gene retired after 50 plus years in the ministry and is presently Pastor Emeritus of the Countryside Baptist Church of Gainesville, Florida. Gene turned 85 on Christmas Day 2017 and spends most of his time writing and speaking.

Gene has several books already available and several in the process. His books are available, both in Kindle format and in print.

Other Books by Gene Keith

You Can Understand the Revelation.

Daniel: The Key to Prophecy

Cremation: Are You Sure?

It's All About Jesus

Religious but Lost

Suicide: Is Suicide the Unpardonable Sin?

Getting Started Right: A Handbook for Serious Christians

Easter: Facts versus Fiction

How to Enjoy Christmas in a World that has lost its Way

Evolution: Facts versus Fiction

Why do Bad Things Happen to God's People?

The Radical Same Sex Revolution

Can a Saved Person Ever be Lost Again?

Otter Creek: True Stories of People and Places

Public School or Christian School?

One Nation Under God - or Allah. Can America Survive?

Financial Solutions (A Handbook for Church Leaders)

Our Story: God is Good- - All the Time!

Stop Changing History

If you would like to order any of Gene's books, go to **Amazon.com, type in Books by Gene Keith** and simply follow the links.

You may also correspond with Gene by email: gk122532@gmail.com.

Made in the USA
Columbia, SC
24 October 2018